Explore
South America

Molly Aloian & Bobbie Kalman

🌳 **Crabtree Publishing Company**

www.crabtreebooks.com

Explore the Continents

A Bobbie Kalman Book

Dedicated by Molly Aloian
For my wonderful friends Vesna, Mandi, and Tanya—let's all go to South America!

Editor-in-Chief
Bobbie Kalman

Writing team
Molly Aloian
Bobbie Kalman

Substantive editor
Kathryn Smithyman

Editors
Michael Hodge
Kelley MacAulay

Photo research
Crystal Foxton

Design
Katherine Kantor

Production coordinator
Heather Fitzpatrick

Prepress technician
Nancy Johnson

Consultant
Dr. W. George Lovell, Professor, Department of Geography, Queen's University

Illustrations
Barbara Bedell: pages 4 (animal), 19, 30 (bird)
Samantha Crabtree: pages 4-5 (map), 7, 26, 30 (map), 31
Robert MacGregor: front cover (map), back cover (map), pages 8-9,
    12 (map), 14, 16 (map), 18, 20 (map)
Vanessa Parson-Robbs: pages 5 (flower), 20 (fox)
Tiffany Wybouw: page 16 (frog)

Photographs
Achim Pohl/Das Fotoarchiv/Alpha Presse: page 29 (top)
Dreamstime.com: Nathan Jaskowiak: page 12
Garry Adams/Index Stock: page 27
iStockphoto.com: front cover, back cover, pages 1, 3, 6, 10, 11 (bottom),
    13, 14-15, 16, 17 (top), 18, 19, 20-21, 22, 24, 31
Carl Frank/Photo Researchers, Inc.: page 28
© Shutterstock: Presiyan Panayotov: page 29 (bottom);
    Michael Schofield: page 11 (top)
Other images by Digital Stock, Digital Vision, Flat Earth, and
    Tongro Image Stock

Library and Archives Canada Cataloguing in Publication

Aloian, Molly
    Explore South America / Molly Aloian & Bobbie Kalman.

(Explore the continents)
Includes index.
ISBN 978-0-7787-3076-7 (bound)
ISBN 978-0-7787-3090-3 (pbk.)

    1. South America--Geography--Juvenile literature.
I. Kalman, Bobbie, 1947- II. Title. III. Series.

F2208.5.A46 2007   j918   C2007-900765-1

Library of Congress Cataloging-in-Publication Data

Aloian, Molly.
    Explore South America / Molly Aloian & Bobbie Kalman.
        p. cm. -- (Explore the continents)
    Includes index.
    ISBN-13: 978-0-7787-3076-7 (rlb)
    ISBN-10: 0-7787-3076-X (rlb)
    ISBN-13: 978-0-7787-3090-3 (pb)
    ISBN-10: 0-7787-3090-5 (pb)
    1. South America--Juvenile literature. 2. South America--
Geography--Juvenile literature. I. Kalman, Bobbie. II. Title.
III. Series.
    F2208.5.A46 2007
    980--dc22
                                                        2007003501

Crabtree Publishing Company

www.crabtreebooks.com   1-800-387-7650

Published in Canada
Crabtree Publishing
616 Welland Ave.
St. Catharines, Ontario
L2M 5V6

Published in the United States
Crabtree Publishing
PMB16A
350 Fifth Ave., Suite 3308
New York, NY 10118

Published in the United Kingdom
Crabtree Publishing
White Cross Mills
High Town, Lancaster
LA1 4XS

Published in Australia
Crabtree Publishing
386 Mt. Alexander Rd.
Ascot Vale (Melbourne)
VIC 3032

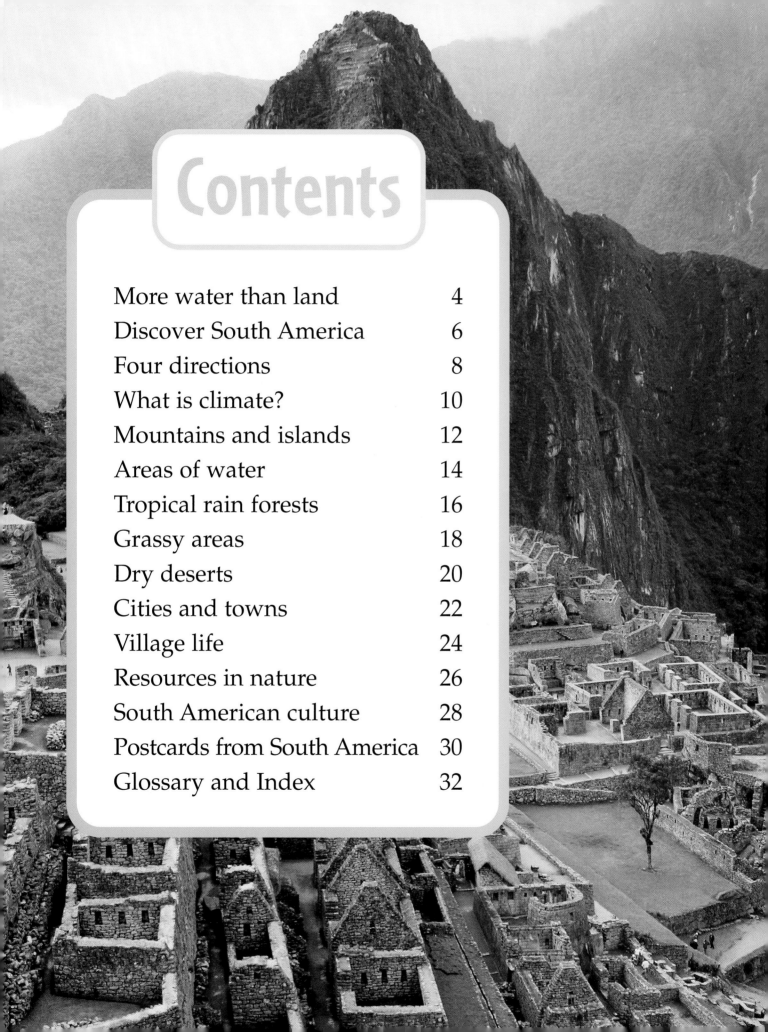

Contents

More water than land

Most of Earth is covered with water. The largest areas of water are called **oceans**. There are five oceans on Earth. From largest to smallest, they are the Pacific Ocean, the Atlantic Ocean, the Indian Ocean, the Southern Ocean, and the Arctic Ocean.

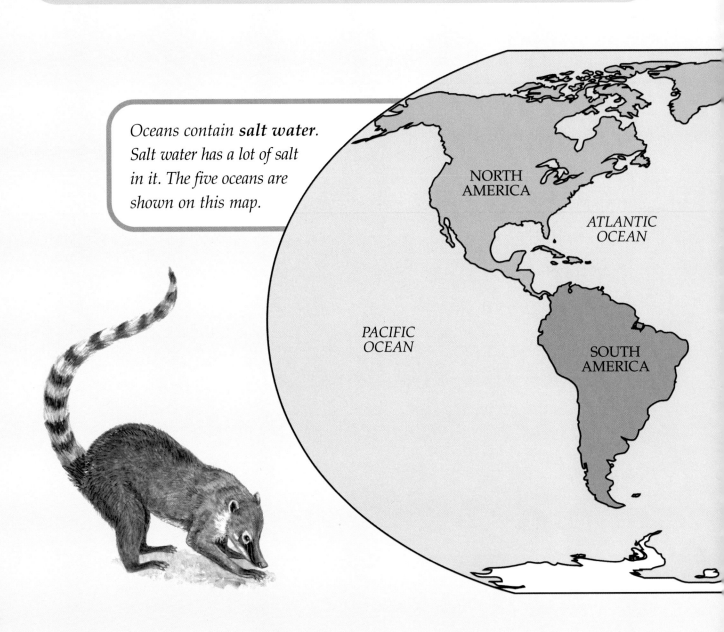

Oceans contain **salt water**. Salt water has a lot of salt in it. The five oceans are shown on this map.

NORTH AMERICA

ATLANTIC OCEAN

PACIFIC OCEAN

SOUTH AMERICA

The seven continents

There are seven **continents** on Earth. A continent is a huge area of land. The seven continents are Asia, Africa, North America, South America, Antarctica, Europe, and Australia/Oceania. Asia is the largest continent. Australia is the smallest continent.

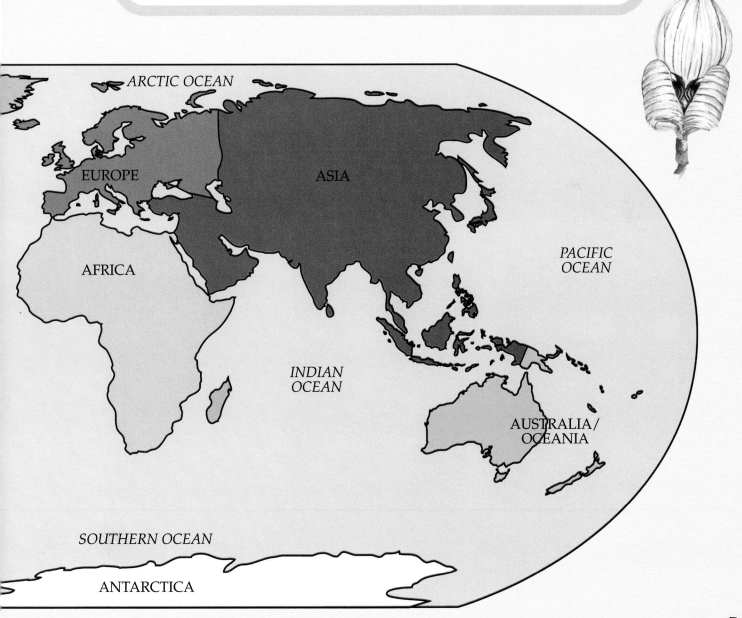

ARCTIC OCEAN

EUROPE

ASIA

AFRICA

PACIFIC OCEAN

INDIAN OCEAN

AUSTRALIA/ OCEANIA

SOUTHERN OCEAN

ANTARCTICA

Discover South America

This book is about the continent of South America. There are twelve **countries** in South America. A country is a part of a continent. A country has **borders** and a **government**. Borders are lines where one country ends and another country begins. A government is a group of people who make decisions for the people who live in a country.

*There are huge **waterfalls** in South America. The waterfalls in this picture are called Iguaçu Falls.*

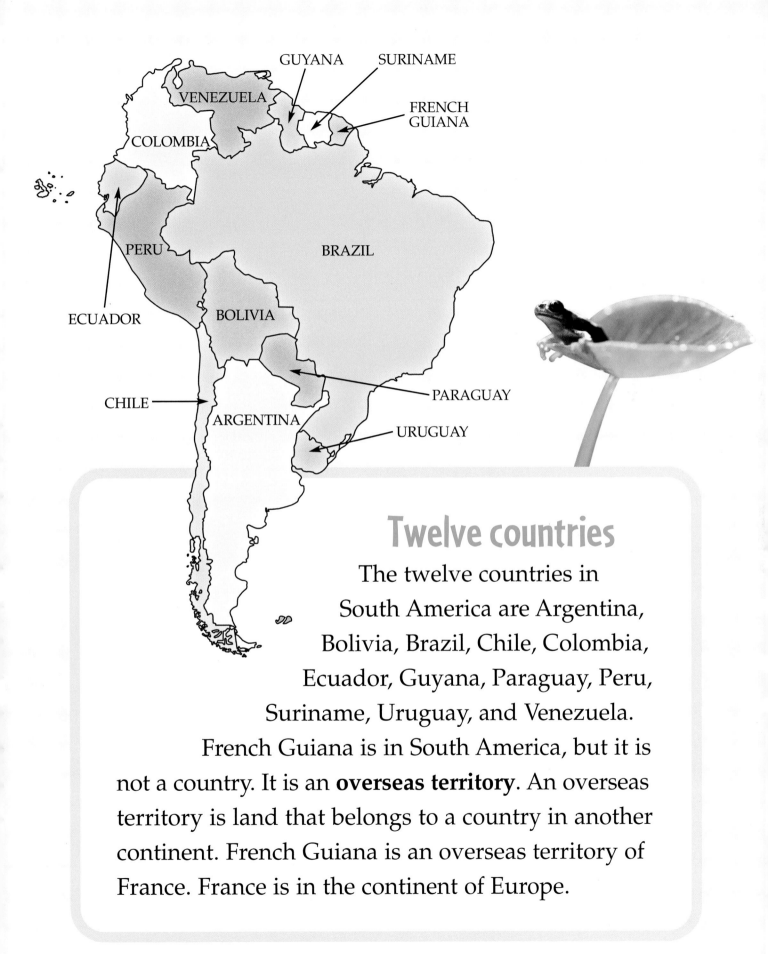

GUYANA SURINAME

VENEZUELA

FRENCH
GUIANA

COLOMBIA

PERU

BRAZIL

ECUADOR

BOLIVIA

PARAGUAY

CHILE

ARGENTINA

URUGUAY

Twelve countries

The twelve countries in
South America are Argentina,
Bolivia, Brazil, Chile, Colombia,
Ecuador, Guyana, Paraguay, Peru,
Suriname, Uruguay, and Venezuela.
French Guiana is in South America, but it is
not a country. It is an **overseas territory**. An overseas
territory is land that belongs to a country in another
continent. French Guiana is an overseas territory of
France. France is in the continent of Europe.

Four directions

What are the four main **directions** on Earth? The four main directions are north, south, east, and west. If you visit the **North Pole**, you are at the most northern point on Earth. If you visit the **South Pole**, you are at the most southern point on Earth. In places near the North Pole and the South Pole, the weather is cold all year long.

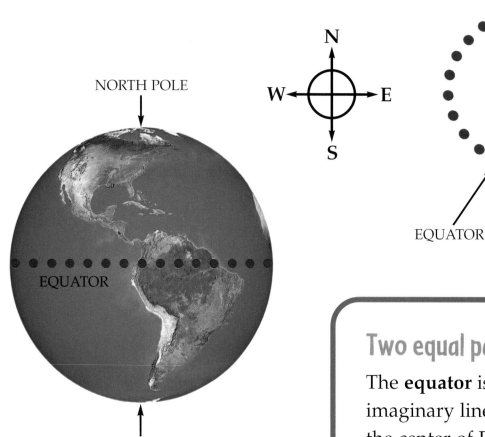

NORTH POLE

N

W ← → E

S

EQUATOR

EQUATOR

SOUTH POLE

Two equal parts

The **equator** is an imaginary line around the center of Earth. It divides Earth into two equal parts.

SOUTH
AMERICA

The northern part

The **Northern Hemisphere** is the part of Earth that is between the equator and the North Pole.

The southern part

South America is in the **Southern Hemisphere**. The Southern Hemisphere is the part of Earth that is between the equator and the South Pole.

What is climate?

Near the equator, the **climate** is always hot. Climate is made up of temperature, rainfall, and wind. It is the weather that an area has had for a long period of time. The equator passes through the top of South America. The areas of South America that are near the equator have hot climates. The areas of South America that are far from the equator have cold climates.

*In the most southern parts of South America, the weather is always cold. Huge, thick sheets of ice cover much of the land and water. These sheets of ice are called **glaciers**.*

Right as rain

Some areas of South America receive more rain than other areas do. In some areas, it rains almost every day. In other areas, there is almost no rain. There are also areas of South America where it rains only during part of the year. The rest of the year is dry. The period with rain is called the **rainy season**. The **dry season** is the period without rain.

This fox lives in a part of Chile that receives almost no rain.

Some areas of Brazil receive heavy rain almost every day.

Mountains and islands

There are a lot of **mountains** in South America. Mountains are tall areas of land with steep sides. The Andes Mountains are in South America. They are along the western side of the continent.

ANDES MOUNTAINS

mountains

The brown areas on this map show the locations of some mountains in South America.

*The Andes is the longest **mountain range** in the world. A mountain range is a group of mountains that form a line.*

Interesting islands

There are **islands** in South America. Islands are areas of land surrounded by water. The Galápagos Islands are a group of islands in South America. They are part of Ecuador. The Galápagos Islands are surrounded by the Pacific Ocean. Animals such as birds, sea lions, and iguanas live on these islands and in the ocean waters around the islands.

Many people travel to the Galápagos Islands to study the animals there.

Areas of water

South America is between two oceans. The Atlantic Ocean is along the east **coast** of South America, and the Pacific Ocean is along the west coast of South America. A coast is land that is next to an ocean or a **sea**. A sea is an area of ocean water with land around it. The northern coast is along a sea called the Caribbean Sea.

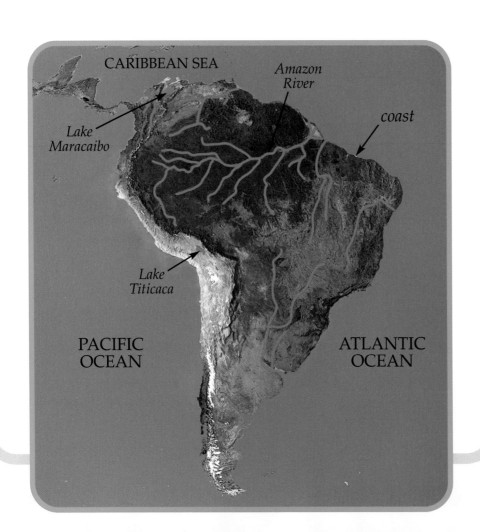

CARIBBEAN SEA

Amazon River

coast

Lake Maracaibo

Lake Titicaca

PACIFIC OCEAN

ATLANTIC OCEAN

*Small fish called piranhas live in **rivers** and streams in South America. These fish live in groups called **schools**.*

The Amazon River

The second-longest **river** on Earth is in South America. This river is called the Amazon River. The Amazon River flows through Peru and Brazil. Over 1,000 **tributaries** run into it. A tributary is a stream or a small river that flows into a larger river.

Tropical rain forests

There are **tropical rain forests** in South America. Tropical rain forests are forests with many tall trees. They grow only in areas that are hot and rainy. Tropical rain forests receive at least 100 inches (254 cm) of rain each year.

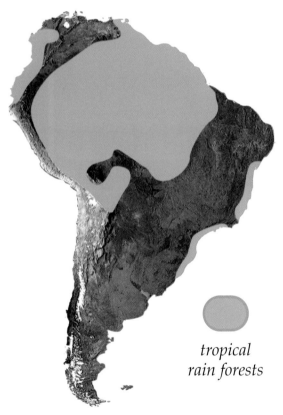

tropical
rain forests

The Amazon rain forest

The largest tropical rain forest in South America is called the Amazon rain forest. This rain forest is the largest tropical rain forest in the world!

This blue morpho butterfly lives in a tropical rain forest in South America.

This animal is a squirrel monkey. It lives in the rain forests of South America.

Tree time

Many kinds of animals live in tropical rain forests. Three-toed sloths live in the trees. Many species of bats, birds, and monkeys also live high above the ground. They find food in the trees.

*Three-toed sloths eat twigs, **buds**, and leaves that grow on trees in rain forests.*

Grassy areas

THE PAMPAS

grasslands

Grasslands are large areas of land that are mainly flat. Many types of grasses grow on grasslands. Some shrubs and a few kinds of trees also grow on grasslands. One large South American grassland is called the **pampas**. The pampas is in Argentina and Uruguay.

*These animals are called capybaras. Capybaras live on grasslands in South America. Capybaras are the largest **rodents** on Earth.*

Guanacos eat grasses and other plants on the pampas.

Grassland animals

Hundreds of animals live on the pampas. Greater rheas, maned wolves, and guanacos are just a few of the animals that live on these grasslands.

Greater rheas use grasses to make nests on the pampas.

Dry deserts

There are **deserts** in South America. Deserts are dry, hot places. Very little rain falls in deserts each year. The Atacama Desert is a large desert in South America. It is more than 600 miles (966 km) long.

ATACAMA DESERT

deserts

Desert animals

Very few animals live in the Atacama Desert because it is so dry. Animals need water to stay alive. A few types of birds, lizards, and insects live in parts of the desert. Foxes also live in the Atacama Desert.

The Atacama Desert is one of the driest deserts on Earth. Some parts of the desert have not received rain for over 400 years!

Desert life

More than one million people live in the Atacama Desert. Many people live in **villages** and towns. Some people are **miners**. Miners dig huge holes in the ground and remove **minerals**. Coal and copper are two kinds of minerals found in the ground.

This woman lives in a village in the Atacama Desert.

Cities and towns

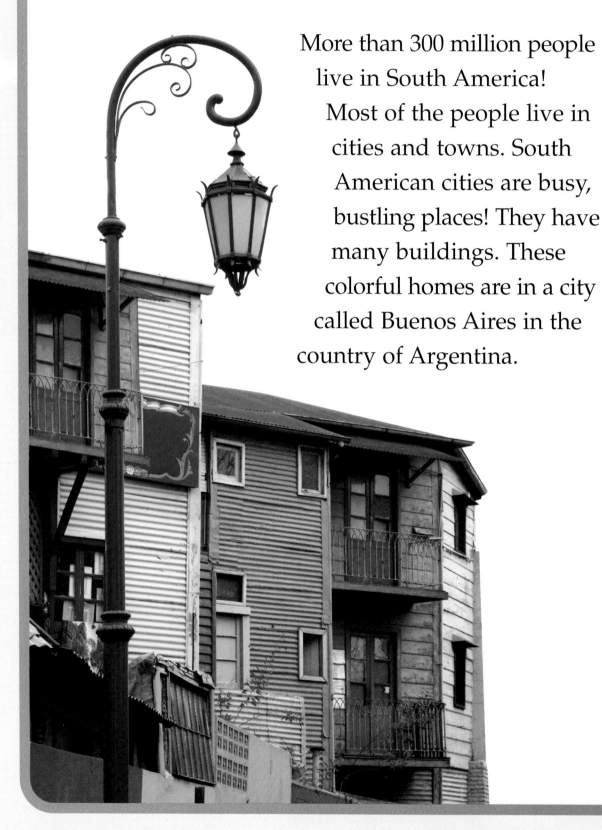

More than 300 million people live in South America! Most of the people live in cities and towns. South American cities are busy, bustling places! They have many buildings. These colorful homes are in a city called Buenos Aires in the country of Argentina.

Millions of people in cities

Many cities in South America are near the Atlantic Ocean or the Pacific Ocean. There are beaches in these cities. Rio de Janeiro has beautiful sandy beaches. Rio de Janeiro is the second-largest city in Brazil. Over six million people live there. People from all over the world visit Rio de Janeiro to see its beaches and mountains and to enjoy the warm weather.

Village life

Many people in South America live in **rural areas** outside of busy cities and towns. They live in villages. Not all the villages are on land. The village in this picture is on a **lake** called Lake Titicaca. It is built on a floating island. The people who live there are called the Uros. The Uros made the island by hand from dried **reeds**, which they tied together. They also made their homes, boats, and furniture from dried reeds.

reed boat

Growing food

Many people who live in rural areas grow fruits and vegetables for their families to eat. They grow fruits and vegetables in gardens or on farms. Some people sell any extra food at outdoor markets, such as the one shown above. People also raise animals, such as cows, so their families have meat to eat.

Resources in nature

Natural resources are materials found in nature that can be sold to make money. South America has many natural resources. Oil, coal, and trees are some of South America's natural resources. Beef, bananas, corn, and sugar cane are other natural resources found in South America.

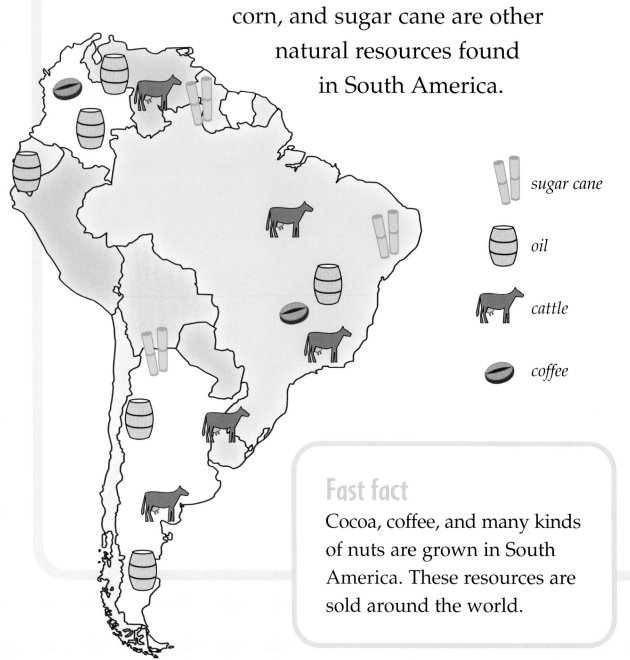

sugar cane

oil

cattle

coffee

Fast fact

Cocoa, coffee, and many kinds of nuts are grown in South America. These resources are sold around the world.

Metals and gems

Gold and silver are other natural resources found in South America. Gold and silver are types of **metals**. Diamonds and emeralds also come from South America. Diamonds and emeralds are **gems**. People can sell these natural resources for a lot of money.

This boy and his father are looking for gold.

South American culture

Culture is the beliefs, customs, and ways of life that a group of people share. People create art, music, and dances to **express**, or show, their cultures. Sports and games are also part of people's cultures. These pages show some of the ways in which South American people express their cultures.

These Aymara Indians live in Bolivia.
The women are dancing a traditional dance.

Playing futbol

Soccer is the most popular sport in South America. Children and adults in every South American country play soccer. In South America, soccer is called **futbol** or **futebol**.

Soccer is especially popular in Argentina, Brazil, and Uruguay.

This girl is wearing a costume for carnival.

Carnival

Carnival is a joyful celebration that takes place each year in February. Carnival includes noisy street parades, colorful costumes, music, food, singing, and dancing. People in South America celebrate carnival for several days.

29

Postcards from South America

There are many beautiful and interesting places in South America. People from all over the world visit these places for fun! People who visit places for fun are called **tourists**. These pages show some of the most spectacular sights in South America. The maps show where the places are located.

There are thousands of animals on the Galápagos Islands. One of these animals is the Galápagos tortoise. It can live over 100 years!

People go to South America to explore the Amazon rain forest. They take **ecotours** to learn about the rain forest and the Amazon River.

In the mountains of Peru, there is an **ancient** city called Machu Picchu. It was built in the 1400s by people called the Inca.

Glossary

Note: Boldfaced words that are defined in the text may not appear in the glossary.

ancient Describing something that is very old

bud A part of a plant that grows into a leaf or a flower

ecotour A trip to visit and observe natural areas and the plants and animals that live there

gem A special stone that can be polished and carved

lake A large area of water that is surrounded by land

metal A hard, shiny material such as gold, silver, or copper

mineral A substance, such as coal, that is found in nature, often under the ground

reed A tall grass that grows in water

river A large area of water that flows into another waterway

rodent An animal with a pair of long front teeth that never stop growing and are used for gnawing

rural area A place outside a city or a town

stream A small, narrow river

village Houses and other buildings that are in a rural area

waterfall A stream of water that falls from a high place

Index

Printed in the U.S.A.